Panic to Pivot
For Leaders

50 Strategies to Move
from
Stress to Strength

Reina Bach

Panic to Pivot for Leaders: 50 Strategies to Move from Stress to
Strength

ISBN: 979-8-218-77921-4

Printed in the United States of America

Table of Contents

Acknowledgements

To my greatest teachers and inspiration, Finley and Connor. Thank you for choosing me as your mom. I love you to the moon and back a gazillion times… and more every day.

Thank you to Amy Miller and Calie Thomas. I'm deeply grateful for your unwavering support and your strong commitment to helping leaders realize their full potential.

To you brave leaders who face storms, stand in the middle of chaos and uncertainty, and navigate the currents of turbulent waters. You demonstrate fortitude and perseverance as you guide, mentor and lead your teams and organizations to success. You deserve recognition for accepting this great responsibility.

Introduction

From Panic to Pivot: The Leadership Mindset Reset

Nothing stays constant. We evolve and our business evolves. You decide how to step into the evolution.

You're likely facing some sort of change (even upheaval) or you're in the midst of it. Maybe you took a promotion and are drinking from a firehose, grappling with budget cuts, managing new responsibilities in your current role, figuring out how to integrate new technologies like AI into your business, trying to win back a lost a key client, navigating global market pressures, or facing some other type of change. What was no longer is, yet you must move forward. Staying still is not an option.

When change hits (by choice or not), it can feel unsettling. You might be saying, "I've got this. We've got this", and at the same time be saying to yourself, "How am I going to do this? Can my team handle this? Do we have the right resources? What if we fail?" Your mind is rapidly trying to reconfigure the new, but something's in the way. This "something" can be a state of panic – mentally, physically, emotionally. You might feel it in your body before your mind recognizes it. The experience of losing control of your life or business operations creates a sudden tightness in the pit of your stomach while your mind races uncontrollably. Your heartrate escalates and your breathing becomes shallower. That's panic mode. Panic mode enters your life through two different methods which start as a gradual anxiety build-up or strike suddenly during important meetings.

I have experienced this situation multiple times throughout my life, both professionally and personally. There were numerous situations where I faced a developing crisis while sitting in my executive position and I had to decide whether to make an immediate call or delay it. The decision point requires you to choose between moving forward or making a change in direction. The decision process requires you to change your thinking approach as much as it needs you to choose your next action.

This book presents a different approach than traditional positive thinking manuals. It's not a collection of motivational sticky notes. This book provides essential guidance for leaders who want to transform their thinking during critical situations that require immediate action.

The fundamental structure of From Panic to Pivot rests on three Mindset Shift Pillars:

1. The ability to recognize proper moments for slowing down allows you to achieve faster progress toward your goals.
2. The ability to move from familiar territory to new unexplored areas requires leadership courage.
3. The process of converting inspiration into concrete actions leads to success.

The book provides 50 specific strategies which help leaders handle uncertainty while motivating their teams and producing results without compromising their personal well-being or ethical standards.

Here's how to use this book:

- The strategies in this book function independently from each other. The book provides complete strategies which allow readers to start from the beginning or access the information they need at any time.
- The leadership approach I present through these pages feels like a casual coffee conversation because leadership work extends beyond professional duties. It's personal. It's you and how you show up.
- Each chapter provides the essential elements of why to use the method, when to apply it and how to execute it for immediate implementation.

Let's launch into the first Pillar - understanding how to pause before you can pivot.

Push to Pause

"Sometimes the most productive thing you can do is rest." ~ Unknown Author

Leadership systems frequently give preference to rapid responses and immediate decision-making. Sometimes as a leader you need to sprint, but effective leadership demands sustained effort over time. The practice of continuous motion without deliberate breaks can leads to exhaustion, compromising your ability to think clearly, generate new ideas, make solid strategic decisions, and motivate others. The most effective leaders understand that fast action without clear direction can give the appearance of progress but often results in wasted energy and purposeless movement.

Taking a moment of pause can seem antithetical to your normal approach. Driving harder, longer, faster isn't always the answer. As much as you might try, you cannot outrun change The solution to every problem does not require additional force. Your success emerges when you take enough time to understand your situation and develop a strategic approach before making your next move.

Pausing does not indicate weakness. It's a strategy. The pause enables you to transition from automatic reactions to purposeful responses through clear thinking, self-assurance and peace of mind. The pause serves as an active state rather than a state of inactivity. It's presence. The pause serves as a vital reset that enables your following actions to become both feasible and forceful.

The strategies in this pillar teach you to develop pause mastery at three times: in the moment, throughout your daily activities, and across your entire leadership tenure so you can lead from your core self instead of from a place of turmoil. The well-timed breather holds the power to transform your leadership approach for both short-term and long-term success.

These 17 strategies teach you to use pauses as a deliberate leadership approach which goes beyond evading challenges. The strategies will teach you to stay focused during turbulent situations while improving your critical decision-making skills and protecting yourself from making poor choices under time constraints.

Push to Pause Strategies 1 - 17

Push to Pause Strategy 1: The Strategic 90-Second Reset Pause

The space between a stimulus and our reaction allows us to make choices about how we will respond. Viktor Frankl stated that we possess the ability to choose our responses after stimuli have passed through a particular space.

You find yourself in a heated business conference. The atmosphere becomes heavy and dense. The room becomes completely silent as everyone waits for your response after someone delivered a harsh verbal attack. Your pulse spikes.

Leadership professionals tend to fall into automatic behavior during such situations only to later regret their impulsive reactions. A sharp retort. A defensive explanation. Your silence becomes a stronger message than any words you could have spoken. Leadership success depends on your ability to remain present rather than your speed of response. The 90-Second Reset functions as your personal leadership reset mechanism.

Your body activates fight-or-flight response when stress levels become elevated. Your body receives a surge of adrenaline which causes your heart to speed up while your thinking ability becomes temporarily impaired. Scientific research indicates that stress chemicals need 90 seconds to process through your system unless you continue to think reactive thoughts. The brief pause enables your brain to transition from panic to clear thinking. Your inner state regains control through this technique which enables you to handle the situation effectively.

When to Use It

♦ In critical situations that require your complete attention

♦ You need to discuss performance with someone who becomes defensive

♦ Your heart rate increases, your jaw muscles tense and/or your breathing becomes shallow

Steps to Practice

1. Take slow deep breaths while counting to four.
2. Maintain a soft grip for four seconds.
3. Your exhalation should last longer than your inhalation at six counts.
4. Continue the process for 90 seconds until the noise disappears.

The most powerful person in the room is the one who remains the calmest. Leaders who learn to pause their responses gain complete control over the entire room.

➥ Action Prompt

How can I use this strategy to shift from push to pause?

How will it benefit me, my team?

How will I know it's working? What will others notice?

Push to Pause Strategy 2: Pause the Scroll, Protect the Mind

Distractions derail. Accomplishing major tasks depends on your ability to avoid minor distractions.

Leaders experience continuous information overload. Information hits from all angles and through multiple sources. Reaching for our phones has become a self-soothing (often unconscious) tactic. No judgment here. But the habit of picking up the phone to seek comfort creates more anxiety than relief. Research indicates digital interruptions disrupt our ability to focus, causing our cortisol levels to increase and compromising our decision-making abilities. That brief moment of "relaxation scrolling" leads to increased stress levels instead of providing relief. Boundaries, bookends around the information coming in is the answer.

When to Use It

- Between your scheduled meetings when your hands automatically move toward your phone
- At the end of your workday when your mental state becomes overwhelmed
- Your brief phone check makes you feel more stressed than relaxed

Steps to Practice

1. Notice the urge to pick up your phone.

2. Place your phone with the screen facing down and activate a two-minute timer.

3. Shut your eyes while releasing tension from your jaw and take a few three deep, slow breaths.

4. Shift your awareness to your physical sensations starting with your breathing, body position and the sensation of your feet touching the floor.

5. After the timer ends you can resume work or use your phone with purposeful intent.

Giving your mind the gift of wellness with breaks throughout the day, too.

➥Action Prompt

How can I use this strategy to shift from push to pause?

How will it benefit me, my team?

How will I know it's working? What will others notice?

Push to Pause Strategy 3: Trigger Management

"Mastering others is strength. Mastering yourself is true power." – Lao Tzu

Stress hijacks clarity. Your nervous system activates battle mode instead of dialogue when emotional levels become intense. Leadership demands influence instead of conflict escalation. Trigger Management asks you to take a deeper dive into developing awareness of what sets you off. To make significant progress so your reactions don't show up uninvited, you need to take a more strategic approach by developing greater self-awareness to create response options. You can still make the same reactive choice, but you are more intentional and more empowered in doing so. Understanding your triggers enables you to better manage them to facilitate your desired impact.

Over time, this strategy leads to changes in your communication style which ultimately transforms your relationships. Given that leaders get things done through others, you and your team will be more efficient by minimizing needless reactions that lead to conflict. Trigger Management can help you foster deeper trust and productivity with your team and others.

When to Use It:

♦ High-tension situations during live conversations

♦ Overreaction to a person or a situation (even an email)

♦ Emotions override clear thinking

Steps to Practice:

1. Make a list at the end of the day of if/when you got emotionally triggered.

2. For each situation, identify the cause of your reaction and how you responded.

3. Every week or two, look at the list and identify themes in the who/what cause with your reactions.

4. For each trigger, identify a specific counterstrategy to rewire the reaction such as deploying the 90-Second Reset. The key here is being aware and intentional.

Make emotional intelligence your super power!

➥ **Action Prompt**

How can I use this strategy to shift from push to pause?

How will it benefit me, my team?

How will I know it's working? What will others notice?

Push to Pause Strategy 4: The Reset Walk

John Muir wrote in his book that nature provides people with much more than they actively search for during their outdoor walks.

The most effective pauses in life occur through movement instead of remaining motionless. Brain research shows that physical exercise reduces cortisol levels while it enhances mental adaptability. A short walk of five to ten minutes will activate your nervous system to bring back mental clarity and fresh perspectives.

When to Use It

- After an emotionally charged meeting
- Before making crucial choices that require your full attention
- You become mentally trapped in a cycle of repetitive thoughts

Steps to Practice

1. Leave your workspace, leave your phone. Step outside if possible.
2. Maintain a relaxed posture while walking at a normal speed.
3. Keep your eyes directed toward the path ahead. Be present. Notice what you're seeing.
4. Follow the pattern of your footsteps by taking three breaths in and three breaths out.

5. Return to work after your thoughts have become peaceful and your mind has cleared.

Move energy to shift and expand perspective.

➥ **Action Prompt**

How can I use this strategy to shift from push to pause?

How will it benefit me, my team?

How will I know it's working? What will others notice?

Push to Pause Strategy 5: Silent Start

The Dalai Lama teaches that silence proves to be the most effective response in certain situations. Leaders who establish their day through silence create an environment of presence and authority. Research indicates that spending ten minutes in silence during mornings leads to decreased stress perception and enhanced decision-making abilities.

When to Use It

♦ Right after waking up before you reach for your phone or check your email

♦ When you face challenging dialogues or experience high levels of stress

♦ Your morning routine becomes hasty, impulsive, reactionary

Steps to Practice

1. Find a device-free area to sit down.
2. Direct your attention to your breathing pattern while keeping your eyes shut. Breathe deeply into your belly versus your chest. Notice the rise and fall of your belly with each breath.
3. When thoughts appear in your mind direct your attention back to your breath without making any evaluation.
4. Continue for 10 minutes (even 5).

5. After your "quiet time" session, write down a single daily goal in your notebook, journal or planner… the one thing that comes in which could be deemed you "next inspired action".

Establish a quiet time practice to center your body and mind.

➥ **Action Prompt**

How can I use this strategy to shift from push to pause?

How will it benefit me, my team?

How will I know it's working? What will others notice?

Push to Pause Strategy 6: The Strategic Stoplight

David Allen states that you can accomplish any task, but you can't complete all tasks at once. And Chris Wahl once said, "You can have it all, just not all at once."

Leaders experience overwhelm because they handle excessive nonessential work. Those who lack clarity tend to view all tasks as urgent matters while treating all projects as essential to their mission. This cannot be reality as some are more urgent, more critical than others. The Strategic Stoplight strategy helps leaders distinguish between essential performance drivers and non-productive activities that waste their time and energy. The strategy provides direct authorization to redirect your resources away from activities which fail to advance your objectives. Your ability to determine which tasks have green lights – your discernment - enables you to move with increased speed, reduced weight, greater clarity and calm.

The stoplight is the visual representation in your mind. Your tasks, projects and meetings exist in three distinct categories which include Green for Go, Yellow for Evaluation (even the need for more data/information) and Red for Stop.

When to Use It

- During both quarterly and annual planning meetings, and during project reviews that produce endless lists of tasks
- You experience multiple tasks competing for your attention

Steps to Practice

1. List all of your current and upcoming projects on a single page (document, spreadsheet).
2. With your team, assign Green status for full speed ahead, Yellow status for evaluation and Red status for complete termination (for now, forever).
3. The team needs to stop the red projects completely instead of just giving them new names.

Free yourself from tasks and projects that don't need your time and energy right now.

➥ **Action Prompt**

How can I use this strategy to shift from push to pause?

How will it benefit me, my team?

How will I know it's working? What will others notice?

Push to Pause Strategy 7: Ask "What's Urgent for Real?"

With the acceleration of change today's world, the statement "If everything is urgent, nothing is urgent" seems to bear even greater importance. Distinguishing priorities is key.

The human brain develops a strong attraction to urgent situations. The fast-paced environment creates an impression that urgent matters are the only way to lead effectively. A frenetic atmosphere can even be alluring to some. The pursuit of false urgency leads to diminished focus (aka "urgency fatigue") and prevents leaders from achieving their actual performance goals. According to neuroscience research, the brain experiences stress hormones which reduce creativity and narrow perspective with the relentless, ongoing sense of urgency. Leaders who pursue every emergency will exhaust themselves and their team members. Leaders who learn to identify authentic emergencies from background noise maintain their energy for handling critical situations.

When to Use It

♦ You experience multiple urgent tasks that demand your immediate attention

♦ Your inbox and calendar start to look like a Tetris game board

- Team members experience burnout because the organization keeps telling them everything has equal priority

Steps to Practice

1. List all tasks which you believe need immediate attention.
2. Select the tasks which directly impact your most important weekly targets.
3. You and your team should feel free to set aside all non-essential tasks.

Your most critical emergencies need your complete dedication.

➥Action Prompt

How can I use this strategy to shift from push to pause?

How will it benefit me, my team?

How will I know it's working? What will others notice?

Push to Pause Strategy 8: Be Here. Be Now.

"Wherever you are, be all there." — Jim Elliot

Leadership positions make it simple to stay absent from the present moment. Your mind constantly shifts between reviewing past meetings, preparing for upcoming ones and stressing about your upcoming big presentation (to name just a few). Your present moment contains the source of your power which enables you to connect with others, maintain clarity and leverage influence. The practice of being present in the moment changes both your leadership approach and how others perceive your leadership.

When to Use It

♦ During individual conversations when your mind starts to wander

♦ During team meetings when outside interruptions try to divert your attention

♦ You experience mental disconnection from the present moment

Steps to Practice

1. Stop and establish a solid connection between your feet and the floor.

2. Perform a single deliberate breath while paying attention to the complete process of breathing in and out.

3. Let go of all thoughts which exist outside the present moment.

4. Devote your complete awareness to the person or work task that stands before you.

5. When your thoughts wander away from the present moment return to the current moment without any self-criticism.

The practice of complete attention will create a better connection and stronger trust between you and others.

➥ Action Prompt

How can I use this strategy to shift from push to pause?

How will it benefit me, my team?

How will I know it's working? What will others notice?

Push to Pause Strategy 9: Brake for Perspective

Author Anne Lamott says that "Almost everything will work again if you unplug it for a few minutes… including you."

Perspective requires dedicated time for its development. The human brain focuses intensely on immediate problems when under stress which helps survival but destroys strategic thinking abilities Thinking narrows, keeping focus exclusively at ground level versus at the 10,000-foot level. And the higher-level perspective is where solutions could be identified.

Your system will reset when you pause, enabling you to view things from a broader perspective. Your brain activates different areas when you shift out of ground-centered thinking, leading to creative thinking that reveals otherwise hidden opportunities and approaches. The action of stepping away from your work leads to enhanced mental clarity.

When to Use It

- You feel stuck or out of ideas
- Your reaction feels sharper than the situation warrants
- You've been staring at the same problem without progress

Steps to Practice

1. Leave your workspace and all related equipment behind.
2. Get active – move. Try walking while stretching, pacing down the hallway, or taking a walk outside.
3. Return with a wider lens and jot down whatever surfaced.

Your ability to see the horizon becomes possible when you expand your perspective.

➥ **Action Prompt**

How can I use this strategy to shift from push to pause?

How will it benefit me, my team?

How will I know it's working? What will others notice?

Push to Pause Strategy 10: Sleep on It (Really)

Exhaustion can compromise sound decision making.

Leadership success depends on sleep as a fundamental tool. And yet, sleep quality is something we take for granted or don't think about. Your brain performs three essential functions during sleep which include chemical rebalancing, emotional processing and information organization that your conscious mind cannot achieve. Research indicates that rest enables people to become more creative while developing better empathy and strategic thinking abilities (plus maintain healthy body weight!) Your ability to make sound decisions decreases when you lack sleep because you tend to become more reactive, develop limited thinking, forego rigorous analysis before making big decisions, and increase confidence in wrong choices.

When to Use It

♦ High-stakes decisions with lasting impact

♦ Emotionally charged conversations

♦ Any situation where you face immediate pressure to make a choice without proper consideration

Steps to Practice

1. Identify the false belief that speed always leads to better results ("urgency bias").

2. Make a conscious decision to handle the matter at the beginning of the following day when you're thinking is fresh.

3. Make sure to get proper rest by turning off all screens and preventing yourself from mindlessly scrolling through information/social media an hour before bedtime. Try to establish a consistent bedtime routine, which tells your subconscious it's sleep time.

The most intelligent choice at times requires you to turn off your computer and take a rest.

↝**Action Prompt**

How can I use this strategy to shift from push to pause?

How will it benefit me, my team?

How will I know it's working? What will others notice?

Push to Pause Strategy 11: The 90-Minute Rule

The human body operates in rhythms throughout the day. We need periods of rest to balance periods of focus.

Performance benefits from scheduled rest periods. Research in neuroscience demonstrates that brain energy levels follow a natural 90-minute pattern of peaks and declines. The human brain performs at lower levels when people fail to respect their natural energy patterns, resulting in decreased mental speed, increased mistakes and reduced creative output. Leaders who take breaks understand human biology better than they think because they use natural body rhythms to their advantage. Strategic time-outs enable you to maintain your mental clarity, physical strength, ability to listen and problem-solve, and emotional stability throughout the entire workday.

When to Use It

♦ Daily deep work sessions where concentration is essential

♦ Long meetings and workshops that lead to mental exhaustion

♦ Projects that need innovative solutions because they require new sources of energy

Steps to Practice

1. Schedule 90-minute work periods into your daily schedule.

2. Take a 10- to 15-minute break following each work period to either exercise or stretch or drink water or clear your mind. Be sure to protect your calendar.
3. Continue this pattern all day without feeling any sense of guilt.

Honor the need of your daily rhythms.

➥**Action Prompt**

How can I use this strategy to shift from push to pause?

How will it benefit me, my team?

How will I know it's working? What will others notice?

Push to Pause Strategy 12: Decision Delay

Strong emotions can weaken decision-making.

Emotion-based choices can result in substantial financial losses, damage relationships and harm organizational reputation. Your brain uses its most basic operating system when you make decisions under intense emotional states. When emotionally triggered ("hijacked"), the amygdala overrides the prefrontal cortex. The reactionary survival emotions of fear, frustration and anger create a narrow field of vision that leads to increased danger from a decision-making standpoint in the workplace. The decision delay enables you to access objective data, peaceful thinking and expert guidance. The outcome produces two positive results: it leads to improved choices and sustainable solutions.

When to Use it

◆ High-risk choices that impact people, financial resources and public image

◆ Intense emotions (fear, anger, defensiveness) are clouding and potentially jeopardizing solid decision-making

◆ You feel overwhelming urgency to decide immediately (when you actually have more time)

Steps to Practice

1. Establish a decision pause by announcing it to yourself or your team members.
2. Acquire new information and different viewpoints during this specific time period.
3. Review your decision after your emotions have stabilized and new information becomes available.

The present pause will cost you less in the long run.

➤**Action Prompt**

How can I use this strategy to shift from push to pause?

How will it benefit me, my team?

How will I know it's working? What will others notice?

Push to Pause Strategy 13: Declare White Space

Leaders must treat "thinking time" as their fundamental duty rather than an optional luxury. ~ Unknown Author

White space serves as a vital element which brings life to creative and strategic thinking processes. Leaders tend to react instead of envisioning when they lack white space in their schedules. A busy schedule appears impressive, but it eliminates needed possibilities for reflection, innovation and adjustment. Your leadership effectiveness depends on protected open time because it enables you to lead from clarity rather than momentum.

When to Use It

♦ During quarterly or annual planning cycles

♦ At the kickoff of major projects

♦ After intense pushes or high-demand seasons when recovery fuels insight

Steps in Action

1. Reserve one to two hours of unstructured time each week in your schedule.
2. Dedicate this time to reflect, recalibrate, strategize and restore.

3. Treat your white space time with the same level of importance as you would any scheduled client appointment because you are the most important client.

Time is a precious resource and so is how you invest it!

↪ **Action Prompt**

How can I use this strategy to shift from push to pause?

How will it benefit me, my team?

How will I know it's working? What will others notice?

Push to Pause Strategy 14: Shields Down Self

How a leader shows up matters. The most effective leaders maintain measured emotions and let their actions generate the atmosphere.

Leadership strength emerges from maintaining neutrality rather than showing weakness. Your ability to stay calm during emotional situations creates an environment of psychological safety that builds trust with your team. I call this the "shields down self" because you drop your reactive defenses to be present in the conversation. Team members feel secure when their leaders avoid taking sides during intense situations because these leaders help the group discover solutions. The use of neutrality during negotiations enables teams to maintain their focus on results rather than personal characteristics. The practice of neutrality helps to reduce intense conflicts (and escalation) by promoting teamwork.

When to Use It

♦ During times of intense conflict when emotions run high

♦ In situations where both parties have strong interests and personal pride

♦ Your presence in emotional meetings determines how the atmosphere will develop

Steps to Practice

1. Recognize your personal biases because unacknowledged biases will control your actions, consciously and unconsciously.
2. Give complete attention to others during their speaking time while refraining from adding your response. Listen deeply, making sure others feel heard, valued and understood even if you don't agree with their stance.
3. When you participate in discussions maintain focus on facts, patterns and solutions while avoiding emotional involvement.

Your ability to remain neutral will guide the room toward productive discussions instead of letting emotional reactions control the space.

➤ Action Prompt

How can I use this strategy to shift from push to pause?

How will it benefit me, my team?

How will I know it's working? What will others notice?

Push to Pause Strategy 15: Read the Room - Pause the Meeting

Trusting and knowing when to pause is a skill of great leaders.

A strategic pause during a meeting demonstrates leadership intelligence rather than weakness. The combination of heated discussions and uncontrolled arguments produces no significant progress but instead results in time loss and relationship deterioration. A read the room - pause the meeting helps teams regain their focus while protecting valuable time and demonstrates self-control to their members. The practice of resetting meeting momentum enables you to establish proper conditions which lead to actual advancement.

When to Use It

♦ During emotional peaks that make discussions unproductive

♦ The situation requires immediate decision-making, yet clarity remains absent

♦ The discussion continues without any signs of advancement

Steps to Practice

1. Stop the discussion to identify the source of tension or unclear points.

2. Establish a new meeting time which will keep the project moving forward while maintaining team responsibility.

3. Return to the discussion with improved vision, peaceful demeanor and concentrated attention.

We all show up with our full selves, including emotions.

➥ Action Prompt

How can I use this strategy to shift from push to pause?

How will it benefit me, my team?

How will I know it's working? What will others notice?

Push to Pause Strategy 16: The Pre-Pause

Thoughtful preparation ahead of time makes all the difference.

Your entry into the room sets the tone for your behavior throughout the space, whether in-person or virtually. Without taking a preparatory pre-pause, the state of mind you bring from your previous meeting or your inbox or general stress levels follows you into the current conversation. A pre-pause practice enables you to lead from a position of clarity rather than being controlled by distractions. A brief time investment leads to major benefits in your ability to lead with authority while maintaining presence and achieving greater impact.

When to Use It

♦ Before difficult conversations or performance reviews

♦ Prior to high-stakes negotiations

♦ Ahead of big decisions where composure matters most

Steps to Practice

1. Arrive a few minutes early p physically or mentally.
2. Take 3–5 minutes to breathe, ground yourself, and set a clear intention.
3. Step in ready, not rushed to bring presence instead of pressure.

Arriving calm changes the entire meeting atmosphere.

➥ Action Prompt

How can I use this strategy to shift from push to pause?

How will it benefit me, my team?

How will I know it's working? What will others notice?

Push to Pause Strategy 17: Celebrate the Pause

Exceptional leaders remember to stop, recognize accomplishments and bask in team renewal before pushing onward.

The corporate world focuses on celebrating launches, milestones and victories but fails to recognize the deliberate rest periods which enabled these achievements. Similar to our own biological rhythms, team achievements have a cadence for success. Part of the cadence is allowing and celebrating rejuvenating pauses as a normal course of operating. Leaders need to catch their breath and recalibrate, teams need to take the foot off the gas pedal for a moment to gear up for the next push. Why not incorporate, acknowledge and celebrate these necessary pauses in service of a sustainable, systemic, high level of performance?

Leaders who publicly recognize rest periods (the "breathers") demonstrate that these moments serve as essential components of their strategic approach. They model the way.

The things you choose to honor will become the standard actions of your team. Your team will experience exhaustion from attempting to produce more output when you only reward their hustle and output. Your team will learn to maintain sustainable performance when you recognize the worth of taking breaks. The practice of honoring rest periods transforms organizational culture by establishing resilience as a leadership quality only enhances clarity, creativity and balance.

When to Use It

♦ You need to recognize the team for taking intentional breaks to generate innovative solutions and make improved choices

♦ The team needs time to recover after completing a major undertaking

♦ You want to demonstrate that restful behavior promotes better organizational standards

Steps to Practice

1. Share with your team how taking a break brought you better results.

2. Recognize the advantages which include improved clarity, creativity and enhanced decision-making abilities.

3. Support team members to try pausing and then discuss the changes they have observed.

The practice of celebrating pauses transforms them into strategic elements rather than demonstrations of weakness.

➥Action Prompt

How can I use this strategy to shift from push to pause?

Reina Bach

How will it benefit me, my team?

How will I know it's working? What will others notice?

Closing Reflections on Mindset Shift 1: Push to Pause

Leadership requires leaders to understand that speed does not equal progress because the world currently values quickness. Leadership success depends on your ability to recognize the right moments for stopping rather than your speed at moving forward.

The 17 strategies demonstrate various ways to implement pauses to circumvent automatic – reactive responses that may not get the results you need.

The common factor among all these pause tactics is their ability to generate power. The practice of pausing helps you regain mental clarity during moments when emotions interfere with your decision-making abilities. The practice of pausing helps you gain a wider view when intense situations limit your understanding and also safeguards your personal energy as well as your team members' operational capacity.

Leaders who achieve the highest level of success understand that continuous motion does not represent their approach to leadership. Leaders understand that rhythm represents true power instead of continuous speed. Your ability to pause effectively will generate more effective choices and improved relationships and enduring organizational success.

Try a strategy. Take that 90-second break. Take those deep breaths to center and regain composure. Delay important choices by 24 hours when it makes sense. The more you pause… breathe… reset, the more time you'll find yourself operating from this empowered state.

Shifting from always pushing to allow a pause serves as a starting point for your journey rather than an endpoint. The following mindset shifts takes you further along the panic to pivot continuum. You will need to leave familiar territories behind to approach unknown terrain.

Known to New

The Comfortable Path Creates a Trap for Leaders.

The established routine of proven approaches, methods, systems provide comfort to people who prefer the familiar – the "this worked in the past, so let's not change it". But holding onto the familiar in a fast-changing world turns into your main obstacle – your Achilles heel. To stay ahead of the competition, other leaders and organizations are pushing the envelope on innovation even when things are working well. Modern leadership requires organizations to go beyond current management because it needs the creation of new possibilities. The transition from established methods to innovative approaches requires deliberate advancement into unexplored territories. This is where breakthroughs and growth occur. The methods in this section will enable you to identify concealed prospects while testing established beliefs, paradigms and boundary limits to drive advancement instead of safeguarding current conditions.

High-performing leaders face a hidden risk because their achievements create protective barriers of expertise which prevent them from seeking outside knowledge.

I worked with a senior leader who had mastered his field during my time at the organization. The leader demonstrated complete mastery of her industry sector and showed exceptional foresight and earned deep respect from her team members. She remained unaware of her current situation because she remained trapped by the familiar patterns of the "known" way her team operated.

The process of determining her future leadership direction revealed her inability to progress. She analyzed all new suggestions through the perspective of established successful methods – current and past. She struggled to shift her perspective into a new way of leading... stepping back, delegating, stepping more into a strategic approach for her team. Her identity was attached to who she was as the superstar with the knowledge. Even her team was hesitant to let her shift into more of a leadership role from essentially a hands-on, working leader.

The process of moving from established methods to new approaches requires you to preserve your established competencies while developing and pushing your outer boundaries and upper limits. The process requires you to maintain your established abilities while developing new capabilities. The process requires you to acknowledge your uncertainty while taking action toward your goals. It's uncomfortable. It's humbling. And it's where growth lives.

You already know how to stop the autopilot grind and make room for fresh ideas.

The time has come to discover the New.

Known to New Strategies 18 – 35

Known to New Strategy 18: Break the Pattern, Find the Gold

Henry Ford said, "If you always do what you've always done, you'll always get what you've always gotten."

Patterns are cozy but left unbroken they prevent you from discovering new possibilities. The pursuit of innovation requires breaking free from comfort zones. Disruption of established routines frees up stagnant thinking and reveals concealed possibilities, enabling you and your team to generate new ideas instead of sustaining existing operations. Breaking up solidified ground enables you to excavate gold that would otherwise remain out of sight and out of reach.

When to Use It

♦ Meetings feel predictable and energy drops

♦ Your "solutions" look suspiciously like last year's

♦ Progress has slowed but no one can name why

Steps to Practice

1. Find one process or practice that feels automatic, predictable.
2. Flip it. Look for ways to change it up… who attends, who is involved, how things are done, which outcomes are measured, how performance is evaluated.
3. Observe the positive effects of disruption and make sure to expand these positive elements.

If we don't look for it, we may not find it. Look for the gold of wisdom, knowledge, connection and opportunities.

➥ **Action Prompt**

How can I use this strategy to move from the known into the new?

How will it benefit me, my team?

How will I know it's working? What will others notice?

Known to New Strategy 19: The "What If?" Habit

Albert Einstein stated that "Logic will get you from A to B. Imagination will take you everywhere."

The leadership tool I find most effective consists of only two words which are "What if?" Simply asking the "What If?" question enables people to move past familiar territory and discover new possibilities.

Your field of vision becomes limited when you experience fear and develop habits. The "What If?" question expands it instantly. The brain's automatic "this won't work" response becomes bypassed when you ask "What if?" This enables fresh imaginative thinking, innovative problem-solving and agile approaches. Leaders who practice asking "What if?" create organizations look beyond the status quo to embrace curiosity and develop both agility and bold new possibilities.

When to Use It

♦ You feel boxed in by constraints

♦ The team becomes trapped in execution details while lacking fresh ideas

♦ Innovation feels stagnant and safe

Steps to Practice

1. Choose a current challenge you need to address.
2. Ask ten different "What if?" questions about this issue while avoiding both judgment and self-criticism. (Hint: one of the questions cannot be "What if this fails?"). Focus on expansion versus contraction thinking.
3. Record all the concepts which emerge during the process. Your breakthrough solution might emerge from these ideas.

Two brief words will reveal the hidden space which you remain unaware of.

➤ **Action Prompt**

How can I use this strategy to move from the known into the new?

How will it benefit me, my team?

How will I know it's working? What will others notice?

Known to New Strategy 20: Environment Matters

The environment plays a greater role in shaping human conduct than people typically understand or appreciate.

Your environment creates subtle patterns that control your actions. The formal atmosphere of a boardroom can elicit posturing and defensive reactions in people. A comfortable environment is more likely to foster an open and receptive reaction in people. When we change what's a typical, predictable environment, our brains create new neural connections which leads to an exploration mindset instead of the usual automatic responses. A fresh environment can support fresh thinking and infuse new energy.

When to Use It

- Meetings feel stale or circular
- Conflict keeps recycling without resolution
- Your team's creativity feels flat

Steps to Practice

1. Take your meeting to a different location by moving it outside or selecting a new area or even a different city. Meet in person instead of virtually.
2. Include participants who normally don't participate in the decision-making process.

3. Try different meeting arrangements by using circular seating, standing meetings and walking discussions.

The solution to progress sometimes requires leaving the current meeting space.

➥ **Action Prompt**

How can I use this strategy to move from the known into the new?

How will it benefit me, my team?

How will I know it's working? What will others notice?

Known to New Strategy 21: Borrow Brilliance

The five people you spend most of your time with determine your current level of achievement according to Jim Rohn.

The fastest method to transition from your current circumstances to new ones requires spending time with people who already exist in your desired future. They are where you want to be.

Your personal growth depends more on your relationships than your acquired knowledge. The people you surround yourself with determine what becomes possible in your life. Find people who operate at your desired level. These mentors will share the keys to their success: mental approach, daily routines and habits, the art of risk-taking, how they make decisions, and more. Armed with this knowledge and wisdom, you will no longer wonder if something is possible because you'll focus on determining when you can achieve it. It's no longer if, but when.

When to Use It

♦ You encounter new goals, skills, technologies, markets that exceed your current abilities

♦ Your present social network becomes too comfortable or limited in scope

♦ Your current environment restricts your ability to progress at a faster rate

Steps to Practice

1. Identify someone already succeeding where you want to grow.
2. Contact them to discuss their work, observe their workflow or work together on a joint project.
3. Apply the knowledge you gain to your current situation by implementing the lessons learned.

Your proximity to brilliant minds will speed up your personal development.

↳Action Prompt

How can I use this strategy to move from the known into the new?

How will it benefit me, my team?

How will I know it's working? What will others notice?

Known to New Strategy 22: Flip the Script

Someone once said, "The most effective choice in certain situations emerges from doing the opposite of what you normally do."

The sequence of your actions determines the final results you achieve in life. The way you arrange your actions determines the type of results you'll achieve. The reversal of your approach breaks established patterns, creating fresh opportunities for you and your team to become more motivated and engaged. A small change in sequence can create the most significant transformation.

When to Use It

♦ During conversations that lack depth and when your standard method produces uninteresting results

♦ You recognize the need to transform team relationships through process changes without causing complete disruption

Steps to Practice

1. Identify your standard first action (your meeting kickoff, problem statement, objectives, goals, mapping out the sequence of steps - anything typical in your approach).
2. Instead, start by asking questions before sharing information and listen to others before presenting your content. Explore different options before making decisions.

3. Observe the changes in energy levels while noting any fresh understanding that emerges.

Flipping your normal approach will open up different possibilities and outcomes

➤ **Action Prompt**

How can I use this strategy to move from the known into the new?

How will it benefit me, my team?

How will I know it's working? What will others notice?

Known to New Strategy 23: Learn in Public

Brené Brown states that vulnerability serves as the origin of innovation. Leaders normally want to understand everything before they start speaking. Leaders believe that possessing answers leads to authority. Leadership achieves its most significant moments by letting go of absolute certainty and substituting it with curiosity.

Leaders who learn in public display their courage, humility and openness to others. It takes all of these to set the ego aside. The practice of learning in public reveals that leadership involves collaborative work instead of individual omniscience. Leaders who show their lack of knowledge gain team trust because they create opportunities for others to join their exploration process. Your display of curiosity gives permission for others to express their curiosity, setting off a dynamic chain reaction of exploration.

When to Use It

♦ You want to bring new ideas into the discussion instead of repeating previous ideas

♦ You want to demonstrate your willingness to accept new approaches

♦ A problem exists which requires multiple voices to solve it effectively

Steps to Practice

1. Share with others the specific question or challenge that you are currently working to resolve.

2. Seek feedback from your team members or audience while refraining from taking control of the discussion.

3. Record the received insights and demonstrate how the team's input influences the final results.

Your team requires better questions from you instead of complete answers.

➤ **Action Prompt**

How can I use this strategy to move from the known into the new?

How will it benefit me, my team?

How will I know it's working? What will others notice?

Known to New Strategy 24: Cross-Train Your Brain – Right Brain Building

The path to innovation emerges through unanticipated connections between different fields.

The most effective solutions often emerge when we look beyond the confines of a limited, systematic problem-solving methodology. Incorporating broader pattern recognition and new knowledge stimulates brain synapses in the right side of the brain. Too often we rely on our left brain in the corporate world. In my experience, this feels more like a "management" approach (looking at hard data, downward focused in the organization looking for efficiency, savings, productivity) versus a "leadership" approach (looking up, out and across the organization and market considering trends, patterns, what's on the horizon). We need both the left- and right-side of our brains to liberate maximum success.

The practice of cross-training develops mental acuity and adaptability, facilitating the discovery of relationships that would remain hidden. Leaders who seek an elevated (sometimes outside expertise) perspective can generate more innovative solutions than those who focus exclusively on their existing knowledge base and experience.

When to Use It

♦ Your mental processes become routine and repetitive

♦ Your team continues to use the same solutions repeatedly

♦ The situation demands an immediate boost of energy and creativity

Steps to Practice

1. Choose a subject that exists in a completely different domain than your current expertise such as art or science or sports or design (even improvisation).

2. Enroll in a class or dedicate time to reading extensively or observe someone who operates within that domain. This gets you out of your typical logical left-brain approach.

3. Implement one learned concept from the experience directly into your leadership activities.

The most significant breakthroughs emerge from stepping into peripheral areas, some that would even seem absurd to the left-brain leader.

➤ **Action Prompt**

How can I use this strategy to move from the known into the new?

How will it benefit me, my team?

Reina Bach

How will I know it's working? What will others notice?

Known to New Strategy 25: Run the Reverse Drill

The process of true innovation requires leaders to question their established thought patterns. Leaders typically believe their existing strategy represents the only logical path toward success. The belief that one path exists can lead to a situation where leaders become trapped.

The Reverse Drill strategy helps you escape the state of inevitable thinking which makes you believe things must stay as they are. The process of exploring opposite scenarios reveals hidden limitations and unperceived dangers and reveals concealed business prospects. Opposites serve as catalysts for innovation through their ability to create new possibilities. The process reveals all hidden assumptions, helping them become visible. Leaders discover new possibilities through the process of thinking about opposite approaches which they would have never found otherwise.

When to Use It

- Your current strategy appears obvious, inevitable and has become overused (even tired)
- Innovation requires moving beyond small adjustments toward significant transformations
- You need to question and evaluate your fundamental beliefs before making substantial financial investments

Steps to Practice

1. Record your present strategy and plan.
2. With your team ask, "What would happen if we needed to reach our goal by completely reversing our current approach?"
3. Collect and analyze the responses to reveal and expand new strategic ideas.

Opposites don't simply attract each other but they create innovative solutions.

➥Action Prompt

How can I use this strategy to move from the known into the new?

How will it benefit me, my team?

How will I know it's working? What will others notice?

Known to New Strategy 26: Invite the Wild Card

The art of independent thinking among diverse groups is what Malcolm Forbes defines as diversity.

The "wild card" discovers solutions that experienced professionals fail to notice. The collective assumptions of insiders create a barrier that prevents them from noticing alternative perspectives. The fresh perspectives of people who come from different work areas, organizational levels and professional backgrounds enter discussions without the weight of established thinking. The unexperienced questions of outsiders generate innovative perspectives which prove to become the solution to complex problems.

When to Use It

- The conversation needs to be interrupted when it continues to repeat unproductive cycles
- Groupthink prevents creative ideas from emerging
- High-risk decisions need outside perspectives to achieve optimal results

Steps in Practice

1. Bring someone who is not part of your usual team into the discussion including entry-level staff and team members from different departments and external industry professionals.
2. Make it clear that their input holds value by giving them actual authority.
3. Pay attention to innovative yet unrefined concepts which originate from outside the typical decision-making group.

The solution to a problem often remains elusive while people are actively working on it.

➥Action Prompt

How can I use this strategy to move from the known into the new?

How will it benefit me, my team?

How will I know it's working? What will others notice?

Known to New Strategy 27: Chase the Tingle

Through our senses and energetic field, the human body detects important information before the brain becomes aware of it.

When new ideas, ah-has, flashes of insight enter the mind, we often feels like a "hit", a small electric sensation that validates the download. You might experience this as goosebumps, faster breathing or heightened alertness. This is your nervous system alerting you to pay attention. There's something here. I call it the tingle.

Leaders frequently choose to disregard the signals their bodies send them. In general, they tend to ignore this signal because they view it as impractical or unvalidated by hard data. Yet, the tingle indicates potential directions which lead people from familiar situations toward fresh possibilities. The instant you detect this signal you will either achieve a breakthrough or let a valuable opportunity slip away.

Inspiration makes its appearance through subtle signals instead of obvious indicators. Your body experiences energy before your brain processes the information. Leaders who recognize and respond to these signals develop their intuition, creativity and innovation skills. Your body sends the tingle as an initial indication that brilliant ideas are approaching.

When to Use It

♦ During brainstorming sessions when evaluating ideas from an energetic perspective, beyond the data

♦ At networking events to save time and energy by checking in with your "internal green light

♦ You want a broader perspective beyond factual information - something that will enlighten your curiosity and problem-solving when considering an idea, making an observation, listening to someone else's point of view

Steps to Practice

1. Stop immediately when you experience the tingle because rushing through it will cause you to lose the idea.
2. Express the idea by speaking it out loud or write it down right away because it might disappear.
3. Return to the idea at a later time to discover what direction the spark wants you to move.

Listen to your gut sense, your deeper knowing.

➥Action Prompt

How can I use this strategy to move from the known into the new?

How will it benefit me, my team?

How will I know it's working? What will others notice?

Known to New Strategy 28: Take a Micro-Risk - a "Notch-Up Risk"

Taking the first, then the next inspired step will move you along the pathway to success.

The fear of failure prevents people from taking action when they attempt to make significant changes. The concept of micro-risks ("Notch-Up Risks" as I call them) presents a unique approach because they create learning opportunities through small experiments that feel secure. This approach teaches your mind and your nervous system how to handle uncertainty without overreacting or getting derailed. As you model the Notch-Up Risk approach, you help your team build this muscle (collectively and individually to create forward momentum. The accumulation of multiple small risks through time creates substantial innovation.

When to Use It

♦ Fear prevents your progress

♦ Your team avoids innovation because they believe the risks are too high

♦ You need to test innovative concepts through small-scale experiments that do not require complete resource (financial and otherwise) commitment

Steps to Practice

1. Identify the idea you're hesitating on.
2. Find the tiniest practical test that will help you validate your concept.
3. Perform the test while collecting feedback to build up your implementation at controlled intervals.

The beginning of every major advancement requires a tiny initial step.

↪ **Action Prompt**

How can I use this strategy to move from the known into the new?

How will it benefit me, my team?

How will I know it's working? What will others notice?

Known to New Strategy 29: Learn from the Fringe

Sometimes the greatest ideas emerge from outside the mainstream.

Think about it. What we once thought of as "fringe" ideas evolved into and shaped the new norm. Who thought of combining peanut better and chocolate before Reese's peanut butter cups? At some point this was a "fringe" idea that is now a popular must-have in some households (at least in the USA).

The fringe demonstrates the ability to transform ideas into mainstream standards. The concepts which appear out of reach present themselves as fundamental elements of tomorrow's standard practices. Leaders who examine the outer boundaries first create change instead of being caught off guard by it.

Innovation develops through the process of experiencing various markets, cultural environments and academic fields. The practice of scanning the edges allows you to detect upcoming trends before mainstream recognition occurs, allowing you to head-off potential competition and give you a market edge. The process of creating innovative ideas requires stepping away from your industry's repetitive feedback loop.

When to Use It

♦ Your ideas feel recycled or incremental

- Your team seems trapped inside industry clichés
- To detect emerging trends and find new business possibilities before they gain widespread recognition

Steps to Practice

1. Read niche publications outside your sector.
2. Follow thought leaders who operate in very different domains.
3. Participate in a conference or event from a completely unrelated field to discover transferable knowledge.

Innovation lives where your normal ends.

↪Action Prompt

How can I use this strategy to move from the known into the new?

How will it benefit me, my team?

How will I know it's working? What will others notice?

Known to New Strategy 30: The 24-Hour Curiosity Rule

Staying curious just a bit longer can lead to better decision making in the long run.

The path between familiar territory and new discoveries exists through curiosity. The practice of delayed judgment creates time for new possibilities to emerge from their closed state. Leaders who practice curiosity create an environment where their teams understand that exploration stands equally important to execution.

When to Use It

♦ Creative solutions need to emerge

♦ Internal and external organizational pressures are rising to cut budget, increase revenue, secure more market share, etc.

♦ Old ways, processes won't move your forward

Steps to Practice

1. Spend twenty-four hours in a structured curiosity phase by asking questions, conducting basic research and creating different scenarios.
2. Instruct each of your team members to do the same.
3. Come back together as a group.

4. After the specified time period review the ideas again to make an informed decision.

Find ways outside of the workplace to fuel your curiosity.

➥ Action Prompt

How can I use this strategy to move from the known into the new?

How will it benefit me, my team?

How will I know it's working? What will others notice?

Known to New Strategy 31: Trade Seats – Trade Hats

Our perceptions of events, situations, others and even ourselves determines outcomes in our lives.

Your ability to view things from different positions whether through physical movement or role changes or responsibility shifts reveals hidden dynamics that were previously invisible. You see not only hidden dynamics, but hidden opportunities, talents, solutions and pathways to success. Shifting where you physically sit in meetings provides a different view. Trading functional hats (as leader, I'm now the executive assistant; as head of marketing, I'm now a plant manager overseeing production of our product line, etc.) If you truly let yourself and your team trade seats – trade hats, you'll be surprised at the insights, understanding and appreciation you experience. Relationships improve, misunderstandings and conflict get sorted out more quickly, and overall productivity thrives.

When to Use It

♦ During meetings that show no signs of progress or when departments create barriers or stalemates to teamwork

♦ You or your team faces difficulties understanding the obstacles colleagues (and/or clients) encounter

Steps to Practice

1. Swap chairs or rearrange the meeting space.
2. Take turns performing different functions starting with leadership duties followed by summary responsibilities and challenge roles.
3. Swap duties for a brief period to gain insight into how others experience their work.

The view from another chair provides the solution you require at times.

↪**Action Prompt**

How can I use this strategy to move from the known into the new?

How will it benefit me, my team?

How will I know it's working? What will others notice?

Known to New Strategy 32: The One-Week Experiment

Short periods of trial transformation can lead to enduring changes.

Short-term experiments provide organizations with both minimal risk and substantial rewards. The approach enables your team to explore new approaches through short-term trials before making long-term decisions. A short period of seven days enables you to discover innovative solutions while finding better operational methods, creating sustained progress toward substantial organizational changes.

When to Use It

◆ You want to explore new changes but don't want to make long-term commitments

◆ Your team needs a creative boost to break free from their regular work patterns and perspectives

◆ You want to experiment and evaluate a new practice, approach with minimal risk

Steps to Practice

1. Identify one practice or process to shift.
2. Establish specific time limits and performance indicators. Identify precise boundaries for the one-week experiment.

3. After running the experiment, collect feedback to determine which elements to maintain and which to drop.

Try new approaches through small experimental periods. You'll gain experience and information to inform decisions.

➥Action Prompt

How can I use this strategy to move from the known into the new?

How will it benefit me, my team?

How will I know it's working? What will others notice?

Known to New Strategy 33: Future-Back Thinking

Stephen Covey teaches us to establish our goals by first thinking about the desired end result we want to achieve, experience, create.

Future-back thinking enables you to break free from current limitations. You create your desired future before establishing the necessary steps to achieve it. The new perspective generates both clarity, ambition and momentum which forward-only planning can fail to produce.

When to Use It

♦ For strategic planning at both team and organizational levels

♦ While facing or in the midst of major career transitions and leadership changes

♦ You feel trapped in short-term thinking relative to professional and/or personal choices and decisions

Steps to Practice

1. Create a mental image of your future self 3-5 years ahead, including both results and emotional states – the what and the why.

2. Record the essential elements which must exist for your desired future to become reality.

3. Start from your present day to determine the essential initial actions that will lead you toward your vision.

Introduce imagination to create a more powerful, unincumbered vision.

➤ Action Prompt

How can I use this strategy to move from the known into the new?

How will it benefit me, my team?

How will I know it's working? What will others notice?

Known to New Strategy 34: Bet on the Bold Move

A Latin proverb states "Fortune favors the bold."

The path to future success may require more than small incremental actions. At times, you are called to make a decisive bet, a big move. Making the bold move demonstrates to yourself, your team and the market your willingness to leap past established boundaries and perceived constraints. The power of bold actions creates momentum, which has the power to attract top talent and generate devoted followership, and surpass the competition.

When to Use It

♦ When you've conducted sufficient testing and your data confirms the opportunity

♦ The only barrier to moving forward is your fear

♦ Your team requires you to make a decision and demonstrate courageous leadership

Steps to Practice

1. Review your list of future plans to discover the courageous choice that you have been putting off.
2. Use data analysis, pilot tests and expert advice to validate your decision until you reach a point of confidence.

3. Establish a specific date for the move and make a firm commitment. Clearly communicate the change to your team and others who need to know.

The safe option maintains your current position. The path to your desired destination becomes accessible through bold action.

➥ Action Prompt

How can I use this strategy to move from the known into the new?

How will it benefit me, my team?

How will I know it's working? What will others notice?

Known to New Strategy 35: Step Back to See Forward

Sometimes you can't see the forest because you're too focused on the trees.

Leadership situations frequently confuse urgent matters with essential ones. The need for fast decision-making leads people to overlook important information, allowing minutia and emotions to cloud their choices. The process of stepping away from a situation enables you to transition from impulsive problem-solving to thoughtful decision-making.

According to neuroscience, the brain achieves better creative information integration through distance because it unites separate elements that seemed distant when you were near the situation. During the step-back pause you gain a broader understanding which reveals both the present challenge of each tree and the high-level patterns of the forest structure. You hold both perspectives simultaneously to see both near- and long-term challenges and opportunities. Stepping back to see forward helps you recognize connections and implications to facilitate greater overall success.

When to Use It

♦ Major financial choices that will impact various groups of people

♦ Managing intense conflicts

♦ You feel compelled to make a choice without complete understanding of the situation

Steps to Practice

1. Establish a specific date for decision-making and share this information with your team members. The established decision date eliminates team members' worry about indecision while providing time for thorough evaluation.

2. Take advantage of the pause to collect diverse viewpoints by asking questions and listening attentively while reviewing all relevant data. Look beyond what's directly in front of you by expanding out into the future, expanding the scope of consideration.

3. After taking time to rest you will approach the decision with new understanding. Your team will learn from your example of patient decision-making while you achieve better results.

A wise leader steps back before stepping forward; the pause expands vision, and from vision comes the decision that truly leads.

➥Action Prompt

How can I use this strategy to move from the known into the new?

How will it benefit me, my team?

How will I know it's working? What will others notice?

Closing Reflections on Mindset Shift 2: Known to New

Change is a constant… and we cannot outrun change. But we can loosen our grip on what was. We can release control of established ways to embrace novel approaches and experiences.

The strategies of asking "What if?", seat-swapping, short-term experimentation and risk-taking encourage leaders to achieve growth through embracing future possibilities instead of repeating past actions. Leaders who choose curiosity over certainty and boldness over safety create new possibilities for themselves and their teams and organizations.

You have entered unexplored territory through your actions, which might include taking risks while testing new concepts and exploring previously inaccessible spaces.

The experience brings an immediate surge of creative energy. New opportunities shine through the night sky with the same brilliance as city lights. Your sense of lightness combines with increased curiosity and a stronger feeling of life. Yet, the sole power of inspiration fails to produce any transformation. The potential of ideas remains dormant without the necessary spark to activate them.

The last transformation holds essential value because it enables people to transition from being inspired to becoming fully ignited. It's about transforming ideas into action. The people who create the most significant impact in leadership and life are those who both recognize possibilities and actively start making them happen.

Your ability to pause and explore the new has prepared you to harness this energy for motivating others, pivoting to the possible, and launching ideas into action.

Inspire to Ignite

The process of turning inspiration into action begins with a spark that develops into a flame of momentum.

The initial spark of inspiration serves as a beautiful starting point, but it's not enough. How many times have you (or someone you know) had a great idea, yet nothing happened? The flame fizzled out… someone gave up too soon, failed to create a plan, forgot to measure and celebrate success along the way to sustain momentum across the finish line, or some other reason.

People frequently confuse short-lived excitement with meaningful transformation and sparks disappear when obstacles emerge. Igniting is different. The process involves establishing conditions which support enduring action, collective strength and resilience. The methods in this section will assist you in connecting your vision to actual results so you can maintain team engagement throughout the entire process.

An unexpected idea creates an electric sensation in the air and even in our bodies. A sudden realization emerges which reveals a potential solution that could transform everything. I love those moments because they create an intoxicating atmosphere of potential. Though basking in these moments is exciting, they need ignition to escape the dream... to release the energy in the forward motion of creation.

If a Ferrari sits in the garage, it collects dust. It's still a magnificent work of art, but no one gets to enjoy what it was meant to do... be driven, appreciated and celebrated.

Leaders who remain in inspiration mode for extended periods accumulate what I term possibility clutter through their collection of sticky notes, voice memos, and extensive to-do lists of unimplemented someday projects. How many times have you (or someone you know) gone through a strategic planning exercise only to have the plan put away in a drawer and never implemented?

This section will deliver an unflinching assessment of what it requires to connect the dots between inspiration and execution.

The process involves creating sparks followed by fueling them until you achieve a successful ignition. Your commitment to ignition will transform everything because momentum will take control while clarity improves. You will develop into a leader who executes big plans instead of merely dreaming about them. You can use these tactics to build bench strength of inspire to ignite team members.

A C-suite leader and her leadership team members joined me in a conference room where flipcharts and whiteboards displayed their excellent concepts. The room displayed high energy levels while people actively brainstormed as the coffee kept flowing. The 90-minute brainstorming session ended, and everyone left with a feeling of inspiration. The team returned to their regular work activities after the whiteboard markers disappeared, and the notes vanished into a forgotten Google drive folder during the following week. Each team member in one way or another got lured back into fighting the fires of the day-to-day. The team failed to advance their revolutionary concepts past the "Wouldn't it be great if..." stage. The realization struck me that inspiration without ignition results in nothing more than idle daydreaming. The experience brings satisfaction but fails to produce any meaningful results.

This section focuses on connecting inspirational moments to actual actions that drive significant changes in your leadership approach, team performance and organizational outcomes. The knowledge from previous sections will guide this process.

You already possess the ability to stop automatic work patterns and create space for innovative thinking. And you've discovered the process of venturing beyond your comfort zone.

The time has arrived to start the ignition process.

Inspire to Ignite Strategies 36 - 50

Inspire to Ignite Strategy 36: Redefine Winning

Maya Angelou defines success as the state of self-acceptance and contentment with how you work and the results of your efforts.

Old success criteria function as hidden barriers that restrict your freedom. Your continuous pursuit of unreachable targets along with self-inflicted penalties for non-compliance with outdated standards will continue to drain your energy. Redefining success enables you to free up your energy while improving your concentration and replenishing your motivation. Establish your own criteria for winning from a more holistic and authentic self-perception that resonates with you. Doing so will fuel your performance as a leader and model the way for your team.

When to Use It

♦ When burnout is high and motivation is low

♦ You experience a perpetual feeling of inadequacy despite your continuous efforts

♦ Your self-worth depends on performance metrics which have become irrelevant to your current position

Steps to Practice

1. Record your present understanding of what winning means to you.
2. Examine if your present definition aligns with your current identity and essential values.
3. Share your updated definition with someone who will maintain accountability for you.

The current game requires you to play according to different rules than those from yesterday.

↪ **Action Prompt**

How can I use this strategy to move from inspiration to action?

How will it benefit me, my team?

How will I know it's working? What will others notice?

Inspire to Ignite Strategy 37: Anchor to a Clear Why

Inspiration can fade, but intention fuels action.

The power of inspiration exists but it remains weak and short-lived without an anchor. Your concept remains a mere spark without a clear purpose. No doubt along the implementation journey, obstacles will appear. Resistance to and from these obstacles can deflate inspiration, take you off course or have you abandon the journey all together.

A strong purpose – a "for the sake of what" – helps you navigate the obstacles, weather the periods of waning inspiration and maintain resilience. Pick a why that inspires you and inspires your team to support you when the going gets tough. The power of your purpose creates an energy that draws people to join your cause. A strong purpose serves as the perfect companion to create a sense of urgency. The combination of your inspired idea with a strong purpose transforms it into an unstoppable fire which affects you and others deeply.

When to Use It

◆ Before beginning any major project, restructuring, product pivot, or other action that will have a significant impact on the team and/or the organization

- When energy is high, but direction is unclear
- You need to share your purpose with others to help them overcome their resistance

Steps to Practice:

1. Determine the immediate significance of the action (or inaction in some cases).
2. Develop your purpose – anchor the why that goes beyond a concept – so you feel the connection to the action and the resulting impact.
3. Share the why anchor in a way which allows others to experience the same sense of urgency, connection and motivation.

Urgency plus purpose drives lasting action and success.

➥ **Action Prompt**

How can I use this strategy to move from inspiration to action?

How will it benefit me, my team?

How will I know it's working? What will others notice?

Inspire to Ignite Strategy 38: Shrink the First Step

The beginning of large visions requires people to perform tiny actions which seem insignificant at first. ~ Unknown Author

Great ideas perish because of inertia rather than insufficient talent or resources. Leaders frequently postpone their initiatives because they want to acquire additional time and data and assurance. This can be difficult in a world when getting to an 80% assurance rate might be the best you can reach. The search for ideal circumstances will result in complete inaction.

The essential thing is to begin with a tiny first step which you can accomplish within twenty-four hours. The process of taking action creates momentum which in turn generates confidence. The smaller your initial actions become the less opportunity you have to create excuses. Any small action you take will create movement that builds.

When to Use It

♦ You're tempted to delay until conditions feel "just right"

♦ The first step feels too big or intimidating

♦ An idea excites you, but sits untouched on your to-do list

Steps to Practice

1. Start by defining your first step before you reduce it to half of its original size. You might consider this your "first inspired step".
2. Check if you can perform this task within twenty-four hours without needing to reschedule.
3. Do it. Don't overthink it.

Start your project immediately by performing the smallest possible action.

➥**Action Prompt**

How can I use this strategy to move from inspiration to action?

How will it benefit me, my team?

How will I know it's working? What will others notice?

Inspire to Ignite Strategy 39: The 48-Hour Rule

The duration of an idea's validity runs out after a certain period of time. Use your ideas before they become useless. ~ Unknown Author

Inspiration creates an unstoppable force which makes your mind race while your energy levels surge. You can see the potential very clearly. The energy from inspiration disappears when you fail to take some kind of action during the first 48 hours. Doubt can overtake rational thinking, transforming the original spark into a mere ember.

The 48-hour time frame serves to sustain the initial spark rather than complete the entire project. The longer you delay starting work the more difficult it becomes to follow the original path because your inner voice will start to dismiss what seemed achievable at first. The spark of momentum develops through taking immediate action (even on what you consider to be a small step). A collection of small inspiration sparks lead to peak intensity and forward motion that can no longer be hindered by unfounded doubts.

When to Use It

♦ You experience the intense mental preoccupation known as "I can't stop thinking about this"

♦ You experience both excitement and fear after waking up with an innovative concept

♦ You understand that postponement will generate additional reasons to delay, a delay you cannot afford

Steps to Practice

1. Select a minimal action that you'll perform inside the 48-hour timeframe. That action could even be: schedule a meeting, draft an outline, send an email, make a call.

2. Record the energy before it disappears since you should take immediate action instead of refining it.

3. Pick your next inspired minimal step and take action.

The fire of inspiration will disappear permanently if you fail to take some kind of action within 48 hours.

↪Action Prompt

How can I use this strategy to move from inspiration to action?

How will it benefit me, my team?

Reina Bach

How will I know it's working? What will others notice?

Inspire to Ignite Strategy 40: Build Your Ignition Team

Someone once said "Action is contagious. Surround yourself with people who move."

Every leader requires an ignition team of a few dedicated people who actively support their initiatives, encouraging and pushing them to take action aligned with stated goals and objectives. Ignition team members are colleagues, mentors and friends who ask, "So when are you starting?" and they keep following up until you execute the plan.

The practice of accountability serves as a force to relieve stress, not create it. Your ignition team supports the shift from inspiration into action. Your chances of taking action increase significantly when you let others observe your progress. Without the team, you can be successful but resistance and doubt may sabotage success. With the right team behind your chances of success multiply exponentially. The presence of an ignition team makes it impossible for inertia to persist.

When to Use It

◆ When projects are identified as essential

♦ High-risk situations require your immediate follow-through because success depends on it

♦ You need people who will support your efforts while providing constructive motivation to help you take action

Steps to Practice

1. Choose two to three people who will both motivate you and hold you accountable to your commitments.
2. Express your concept and time frame to them.
3. Share progress updates and show appreciation for their time, energy, support and wisdom.

Create your dream team. Be on someone else's dream team, too!

➤Action Prompt

How can I use this strategy to move from inspiration to action?

How will it benefit me, my team?

How will I know it's working? What will others notice?

Inspire to Ignite Strategy 41: Prototype, Don't Perfect

Sheryl Sandberg states that completion of work is superior to achieving perfection.

The pursuit of perfection can lead to procrastination and action paralysis. The truth? Flawless never arrives. Countless concepts remain trapped in notebooks – drafted, redrafted again and again - because their creators seek absolute perfection.

The initial stage requires momentum to be more important than achieving mastery. The development of ideas depends on creating a prototype, a beta on the road to getting better versions over time. Real-world data becomes available through prototypes which provide fast results. The testing process reveals which elements succeed, which fail and which elements hold the greatest importance. This approach helps people to stop wasting time on prolonged preparation that only appears to be advancement.

When to Use It

♦ You're caught in an endless loop of your work needing additional preparation
♦ Your exciting concept gets stuck because you fear others will judge you

♦ Your team requires progress rather than additional draft versions

Steps to Practice

1. Determine the most basic version of your concept which you can validate through testing.
2. Present your work to a small group of trusted people who will serve as your pilot audience.
3. Collect feedback from users before you start making changes to advance your project.

Perfection stalls. Prototypes spark.

➥ Action Prompt

How can I use this strategy to move from inspiration to action?

How will it benefit me, my team?

How will I know it's working? What will others notice?

Inspire to Ignite Strategy 42: Pair Inspiration with Deadline

Inspiration becomes meaningless when it lacks execution. ~ Unknown Author

The excitement of inspiration fades away when there is no deadline to work toward. The absence of a specific date causes ideas to drift away into the realm of future plans, of "some-day". The establishment of deadlines at any level creates an immediate sense of importance.

Deadlines help people to stay focused. The process of tuning into inspiration and developing innovative ideas remain protected from being lost in the chaos of daily tasks. Linking inspiration to a specific date enables you to transform it into a concrete goal that requires accountability. The power of deadlines is that priorities are identified and sorted, delayed decisions finally get made, actions big and small get taken and dreams become reality.

When to Use It

♦ Any situation where an idea remains stuck in development
♦ To transition from endless planning to actual production work is critical
♦ To transform your abstract goals into concrete achievements

Steps to Practice

1. Select a significant achievement point that represents your concept.
2. Establish a deadline which should be inspiring yet avoid being too challenging or stressful.
3. Inform someone who will provide encouragement or maintain your commitment.

A deadline serves as the catalyst which turns inspirational ideas into actual progress.

➥Action Prompt

How can I use this strategy to move from inspiration to action?

How will it benefit me, my team?

How will I know it's working? What will others notice?

Inspire to Ignite Strategy 43: Name the Win

The achievement of success remains impossible when you fail to establish its definition. ~ Unknown Author

Leaders who begin projects without clear success definitions end up working endlessly without any signs of advancement. The solution to this problem requires defining success goals before digging into the work. The definition of success needs to be specific and concrete.

The process of achieving clear goals helps you stay focused while maintaining motivation levels. The establishment of clear wins helps organizations avoid project expansion while reducing feelings of overwhelm, enabling team members to experience the fulfilling experience of completing their work. The absence of defined success criteria leads people to mistake their work activities with actual achievements. Busy-ness itself isn't the win.

When to Use It

♦ Before investing serious time or resources
♦ The beginning of new initiatives, projects and campaigns to promote clarity
♦ Any time momentum feels fuzzy or unmeasurable

Steps to Practice

1. Ask: What will tell me we've succeeded, specifically?
2. Define it in observable terms (e.g., "first customer signed" vs. "worked on it for a while").
3. Share the win with your team so everyone is aiming for the same target.

The process of achieving goals becomes visible when we establish clear definitions, making success worth celebrating.

➤ **Action Prompt**

How can I use this strategy to move from inspiration to action?

How will it benefit me, my team?

How will I know it's working? What will others notice?

Inspire to Ignite Strategy 44: Leverage Momentum Windows

The timing of everything matters because it has the power to transform all situations.

Every period in time possesses distinct qualities including focused attention, courageous determination and precise decision-making abilities. Leaders who understand how to identify momentum windows achieve better results with speed and effectiveness than others who attempt to work through their weakest moments.

Your energy levels work with momentum windows to create positive results. Your natural high points become more powerful when you perform important tasks at those times because they enhance both your stamina mental clarity. High-stakes work performed during low-energy periods will increase the chances of hesitation and compromise quality.

When to Use It

- Situations that need courage, boldness and major choices
- You discover specific times when your creativity, focus and fearlessness become more pronounced
- High-stakes work needs your peak energy

Steps to Practice

1. Observe the specific times when you achieve your highest levels of energy, confidence and mental clarity. (maybe at your best you're an early morning person or a late night person)
2. Reserve those specific time slots for critical decisions, initial actions and important presentations.
3. Defend this time period as if it were your most vital business appointment. Protect your calendar.

The effectiveness of any action diminishes when performed at an inappropriate time.

➤ **Action Prompt**

How can I use this strategy to move from inspiration to action?

How will it benefit me, my team?

How will I know it's working? What will others notice?

Inspire to Ignite Strategy 45: Turn "What If" into "What Now"

Inspiration sparks curiosity, which fuels solution generation and forward action.

The starting point of inspiration emerges from asking "What if?" This question opens up space to generate new creative ideas, fresh perspectives and potential solutions. The "What if" state creates a protective bubble to encourage, foster and enhance innovation.

The second part of the recipe for success is to shift from idea generation into idea in action.

The transition from dreaming to taking action happens when you ask yourself "What now?" The powerful combination of "What if?" and "What now?" enables possibility expansion and generates actual progress. The practice of asking "What now?" helps you break free from getting overwhelmed with possibilities to generate real progress. This strategy prevents people from mistaking brainstorming activities with actual progress.

When to Use It

♦ You notice yourself repeating an idea without achieving a resolution

- Following brainstorming sessions which generate exciting yet incomplete results
- Whenever creative thinking reaches its peak but actual progress remains stagnant

Steps to Practice

1. Record your most promising "What if" concepts.
2. Select one idea and then ask, "What now?" immediately. Be careful not to get lured back into brainstorming "What if?" mode.
3. Start with a minimal action to verify or progress the concept.

The phrase "What if?" generates visionary ideas yet "What now?" initiates progress.

➼ Action Prompt

How can I use this strategy to move from inspiration to action?

How will it benefit me, my team?

How will I know it's working? What will others notice?

Inspire to Ignite Strategy 46: Celebrate Early Sparks

Each big win is comprised of many micro-wins.

Leaders tend to delay their celebrations until they reach the end points, but this approach neglects opportunities along the way to boost morale, enhance engagement, fuel momentum, elevate performance and avoid team burnout. The development of momentum starts from initial sparks rather than the end result. The first outreach email. The first rough draft. The first "yes" from someone else. These achievements serve as evidence that progress is underway.

Motivation requires development through effort rather than appearing through chance. Your team and brain will recognize progress through small win celebrations which demonstrate that advancement continues during challenging times. The practice of acknowledging achievements creates a positive feedback loop which strengthens your determination and that of your team to forge (leap!) onward.

When to Use It

♦ At the start of new projects to maintain initial momentum

♦ During the challenging middle phase when initial excitement fades and routine work begins

◆ Process becomes difficult to see and team energy levels decrease

Steps to Practice

1. Define what early sparks look like (first draft, first outreach, first yes, etc.).
2. Establish a recognition practice through scheduled team meetings and individual self-reflection sessions.
3. Treat small victories as essential progress markers instead of being dismissed as unimportant achievements.

The initial sparks maintain the flame until the large fire becomes dominant.

➥ Action Prompt

How can I use this strategy to move from inspiration to action?

How will it benefit me, my team?

How will I know it's working? What will others notice?

Inspire to Ignite Strategy 47: Cut the Deadwood

Someone once said, "The best course of action requires eliminating unnecessary elements."

Leadership roles require leaders to manage multiple dead projects, outdated commitments and goals, all of which have lost their purpose or have a diminishing link to the overarching strategic plan. These initiatives are flat and need to fall off the radar. All the time, energy and resources being invested in these initiatives prevent essential matters from receiving proper attention.

The key to ignition does not depend on starting something new, but rather clearing space to free up attention and action for emerging and important initiatives. It can be difficult to let go of old priorities that don't serve the desired future state, whether it's you holding on, your team or your stakeholders. The process of examining and eliminating outdated projects and unproductive tasks and replacing them with essential, forward-focused initiatives is vital leadership success practice. Cutting deadwood allows you to redirect precious resources to what matters now and into the future.

When to Use It

♦   You experience excessive workload before beginning any work

- Your schedule is full, but you achieve minimal results
- You cannot handle additional responsibilities because your workload already exceeds your capacity

Steps to Practice

1. List all your current commitments and projects – for you, for your team.
2. Identify which are aligned, which are optional, and which are dead weight.
3. Pause, delegate, or stop what no longer serves your (and your team's) highest goals.

The process of clearing space opens space for new beginnings, new possibilities.

➥ **Action Prompt**

How can I use this strategy to move from inspiration to action?

How will it benefit me, my team?

How will I know it's working? What will others notice?

Inspire to Ignite Strategy 48: Build Ignition Rituals

Luck is where opportunity meets preparedness. ~ Roman philosopher Seneca

The rhythm of rituals builds habits and habits are the foundation of readiness.

Leaders understand that the most challenging aspect of leadership begins with taking the initial step. The initial movement toward change resembles an attempt to push against an unyielding barrier. But rituals lower the barrier. The brain receives a signal from these rituals – these practices - which indicates the time has come to begin.

Rituals - practices reduce friction. The process of starting work becomes automatic through rituals which bypass procrastination to generate momentum. The brain learns to use the ritual as a signal to take action through repeated practice. The more you practice, the more you embody the rhythm of momentum toward implementation of an inspired idea.

When to Use It

♦ Starting tasks becomes more difficult than expected
♦ The same area of resistance continues to appear

♦ You need to maintain consistent momentum

Steps to Practice

1. Identify one task where you often stall.
2. Develop a brief ritual – a practice which includes music, movement or breathing techniques or a personal motivational phrase. This anchors in the practice at the physical, emotional and mental levels, supporting greater success.
3. Perform the ritual repeatedly until your brain links the practice to progress.

Rituals serve as a starting point for both work activities and personal development.

➤ **Action Prompt**

How can I use this strategy to move from inspiration to action?

How will it benefit me, my team?

How will I know it's working? What will others notice?

Inspire to Ignite Strategy 49: Keep the Flame Visible and In Conversation

If you want forward movement, keep your sight on the ball and the goal.

The death of an idea stems from its disappearance from public view rather than its inherent quality. The absence of visibility leads to mental forgetfulness which results in complete inaction. Out of sight, out of mind. The visibility of an idea – a goal determines its survival. The flame of an idea – a goal requires constant visibility to remain alive.

Visibility is fuel. Daily exposure to your commitments (and those of your team) helps you remember their value which motivates you to stay active, in motion (and your team). The transformation from "I'll get to it" to "I'm on it" occurs through this method… for you as the leader and for your team members.

When to Use It

- For long-term projects where energy fades over time
- When you or your team lose sight of priorities
- Anytime a high-stakes idea risks slipping into the background

Steps to Practice

1. Place your essential initiative in a spot where you will encounter it every day such as a wall or whiteboard or monitor sticky note. For your team, create a visual to share.
2. The energy will stay alive through visual indicators such as progress trackers, bold reminders and images.
3. Show the information to your team members so they can view it as well. Talk about the progress in team meetings.

The fire continues to burn when the flame remains visible.

➤ **Action Prompt**

How can I use this strategy to move from inspiration to action?

How will it benefit me, my team?

How will I know it's working? What will others notice?

Inspire to Ignite Strategy 50: End with a Launch and a Lunch

The light of day transforms dreams into action and into existence.

Every project requires a completion point which serves as a milestone for delivering your work and that of your team to the world. The completion point should mark the moment when you release your creation (and/or that of your team) into the world by saying "Here it is." Even if the project continues to evolve through improvement cycles beyond the initial complete, mark the milestone.

The launch demonstrates and celebrates the joint efforts of you and your team to your stakeholders and the outside world. "We did it!" The launch brings an end to the project while generating forward motion and establishing trust with others. And because I'm a French chef, I say celebrate with a lunch! Food brings people together, breaking bread even if virtually as you celebrate will foster camaraderie, appreciation and connection... for now and for future endeavors as a team.

When to Use It

♦   The minimum viable version reaches completion

- The fear of taking action becomes greater than the fear of inaction
- Any time your concept reaches a level where you can test it in actual circumstances

Steps to Practice

1. Establish your launch point, big or small. This could be a party, a demo, a presentation or even an email announcement to stakeholders.
2. Choose a specific date for your launch and maintain your commitment to it. Make sure the team is on board.
3. Honor the launch process. Your team will feel a sense of fulfillment with their contribution to the process.

The launch serves as a starting point rather than an ending point. The real value emerges from the initial step.

↪**Action Prompt**

How can I use this strategy to move from inspiration to action?

How will it benefit me, my team?

How will I know it's working? What will others notice?

Closing Reflections on Mindset Shift 3: Inspire to Ignite

Leadership transforms into actual results when a person reaches the point of ignition. Your journey has led you to discover your purpose while dividing major tasks into smaller steps, establishing accountability systems, and starting before achieving perfection. The strategies in this book exist to help you move beyond doubt and achieve tangible advancement because actual change occurs through intention plus action.

Your actions will reveal a fundamental truth about ignition because it requires multiple small actions instead of one major jump. The process of creating forward motion requires small consistent sparks that build up power to light the way. Your progress as a leader who achieves results will grow through the practice of celebrating small accomplishments, establishing rituals, and making your achievements visible.

Your vision will become reality through continuous ignition after you learn to pause and adopt new ways of thinking. You have progressed from Pause to Choosing the New and from Inspiration to full-on Ignition. Your leadership has evolved from thinking, dreaming and speaking to actual movement. Leadership exists in the act of moving forward.

You have mastered the ability to pause without guilt, developed the skill to enter new situations with confidence, learned to create meaningful change through action.

The moment you light a match you will never forget the sight of the resulting flame.

Closing Reflections

Your investment in this book has led you to develop a fresh approach for interacting with yourself and your team and your life.

The three mindset pillars have allowed you to practice the ability in our fast-paced, reactive society to pause, to expand your perspective, and to take bold action in the face of change. The first pillar of Push to Pause demonstrated that leadership power emerges from deliberate intentional decision-making rather than continuous (sometimes unconscious) activity. The second pillar of Known to New showed you that genuine development emerges through pattern-breaking activities which lead to new questions and the willingness to embrace potential. The third pillar of Inspire to Ignite demonstrated how small sparks can activate transformation by moving you from conceptualization to practical execution. These three mindset pillars unite to create a solid suite of strategies to calibrate a leadership pattern which you can use repeatedly in all situations.

The world requires leaders who can pivot instead of leaders who only manage panic, who can pivot because they choose to lead through presence, vision and action instead of fear. Your leadership pivots need not be dramatic to create meaningful change. Your pauses, fresh viewpoints and sparks of inspiration create expanding waves that affect your team members, your organization and your community. You have the opportunity to turn disruptions into opportunities for transformation rather than just enduring them. Through resilience and renewal, your legacy will expand its reach with your ability to shift from panic to pivot to action.

Pick one strategy from this book. Just one. Use this strategy during the current week. Select any strategy without hesitation and apply it right away. Observe the outcome that emerges from your actions. The results will guide your progress. Then, choose another. And another.

Life will continuously present you with chances to pivot through both positive and challenging situations. You hold the power to select which opportunities you will pursue and how you will react to them while shaping the narrative of your future.

Stay Calm and Pivot On!

About the Author

Reina Bach is an executive coach, leadership consultant, and keynote speaker who specializes in helping leaders and teams navigate disruption with clarity, resilience, and strength. Over the past three decades, she has guided executives, entrepreneurs, and organizations through some of their most challenging pivots, teaching them how to transform stress into strategy and fear into possibility.

Reina is the creator of the *Panic to Pivot*™ framework, a practical and proven system that equips leaders to pause under pressure, break free from old patterns, and ignite action with confidence. She is also the founder of *Sensory Living*™, a movement dedicated to helping people reconnect with presence, energy, and joy in both work and life.

With a unique blend of consulting expertise, Gestalt equine coaching, and a background as a French-trained chef and Executive Sommelier, Reina brings a multidimensional perspective to leadership and life. She is passionate about helping leaders not only achieve results but also create lives and organizations that feel aligned, meaningful, and alive.

For more information on my speaking and consulting programs, please contact me at:

Reina@ReinaBach.com

Connect with me!

LinkedIn: www.linkedin.com/in/reinabach/

Website: www.ReinaBach.com

www.ingramcontent.com/pod-product-compliance
Lightning Source LLC
Chambersburg PA
CBHW031436270326
41930CB00007B/736